TWO CONCEPTS OF LIBERTY

By Isaiah Berlin (1958)

More books you might be interested in:

ECONOMIC CALCULATION IN THE SOCIALIST COMMONWEALTH: A critique of the non-existent price system of the centralized communist economy

By Ludwig von Mises

Key points of the essay:

1. Negative freedom:

Defined as freedom from interference by others.

It refers to the question, "What is the area within which an individual can act without being hindered by others?"

It emphasizes the importance of a private sphere safeguarded from external control, a principle advocated by thinkers such as Mill, Locke and Constant.

It advocates limiting interference in order to preserve individual autonomy, often justified by the need for personal development or the prevention of social chaos.

Criticism:

- Negative freedom is not intrinsically linked to democracy.
- It can coexist with autocratic regimes, provided that individuals enjoy significant personal freedom within prescribed limits.

2. Positive freedom:

Defined as self-mastery or the ability to be master of oneself.

It explores the question, "Who governs me? Do I act for myself or for the general good?" or "Who decides what I should do?"

It derives from the desire for autonomy and rational control of one's own life, which distinguishes human beings from animals or passive objects.

Often linked to collective or higher ends, where the "real self" is aligned with rationality, leading to the justification of coercion in the name of "true freedom".

Criticism:

- The concept can lead to authoritarianism when individuals are coerced "for their own good".
- The division of the self into "superior" and "inferior" raises ethical dilemmas regarding autonomy and control.

3. Historical and social context:

Negative freedom is associated with the emergence of individualism and modern liberalism.

Positive freedom is often aligned with collective ideologies, such as nationalism or totalitarian regimes, which seek to liberate individuals by subordinating them to collective goals.

4. The dangers of positive liberty:

The emphasis of positive freedom on self-realization can justify the imposition of values by an elite or a state, which claim to act in the "true" interest of individuals.

Berlin criticizes it as a "monstrous impersonation" that risks eroding authentic freedom by equating imposed will with self-determination.

5. Retreat to the Inner Citadel:

Berlin criticizes strategies in which individuals withdraw from their personal desires to pursue greater external comforts.

Such self-denial may achieve personal serenity, but it cannot be equated with true freedom.

6. The quest for status:

Berlin examines how demands for freedom often merge with desires for status and equality. Status (the need to be recognized by others) is distinct from the essence of freedom.

7. Philosophical and practical implications:

Berlin concludes that the interplay between negative and positive freedom illustrates the fundamental tensions of political thought and human aspirations.

Balancing these concepts requires vigilance to prevent one from undermining the other.

Summary of the key concepts of the 8 Chapters of "Two Concepts of Freedom", by Isaiah Berlin:

Negative freedom: Freedom from interference

In the chapter on negative freedom, Berlin presents the idea of freedom as non-interference. This form of freedom addresses the question, "What is the sphere within which an individual can act without being hindered by others?" Negative freedom emphasizes the creation of a private sphere in which individuals can make decisions without external coercion. Berlin argues that thinkers such as John Stuart Mill and John Locke cherished this ideal, considering it essential for personal growth and the prevention of social chaos. However, he also recognizes the limits of negative liberty; it requires compromises and boundaries to prevent the unbridled actions of one individual from infringing on the liberties of another. The practical value of negative liberty lies in its ability to safeguard individual autonomy while accommodating the necessary constraints of law and governance. However, Berlin cautions that this form of freedom, while celebrated in liberal democracies, can exist in authoritarian regimes if they allow a wide margin of personal liberty within a controlled framework.

Positive freedom: Freedom as self-mastery

The concept of positive freedom shifts the focus from external interference to internal control, asking the questions, "Who governs me? Do I act for myself or for the common good?" Positive freedom is rooted in the desire for self-mastery and autonomy, in which individuals aspire to align their actions with their rational will. Berlin traces this idea through philosophical traditions that emphasize the division between the "higher self" (rational and moral) and the "lower self" (impulsive and irrational). Although positive freedom aspires to free individuals from internal and external domination, it carries significant risks. When interpreted as aligning individuals with their "true" self, positive liberty can be used to justify coercion in the name of the greater good. Berlin criticizes it as a dangerous path to authoritarianism, where rulers claim to know the true interests of individuals better than the individuals themselves. The appeal of positive liberty lies in its potential for self-realization and collective purpose, but it must be moderated to avoid infringing on personal autonomy.

Retreat to the Inner Citadel

Berlin criticizes one philosophical response to the limitations of reality: the retreat into an inner domain of thought and will. When faced with insurmountable obstacles, individuals may withdraw from their desires and embrace self-denial, limiting their aspirations to what is attainable. This Stoic approach, often found in ascetic and quietist traditions, seeks liberation by redefining freedom as independence from desires and external forces. Berlin argues that while this strategy may provide personal serenity, it does not constitute genuine freedom. On the contrary, it represents a contraction of life's possibilities, where freedom becomes synonymous with self-imposed isolation. Such a retreat may safeguard individual integrity, but it fails to engage with the broader social and political dimensions of freedom, ultimately reducing it to mere survival within restricted confines.

Self-realization

In the chapter on self-realization, Isaiah Berlin explores the concept of freedom as the realization of one's true nature or potential. Rooted in rationalist traditions, this idea frames freedom not as freedom from interference, but as alignment of actions with rational or moral principles. Self-realization involves transcending immediate desires to pursue higher goals, in which external constraints are reinterpreted as opportunities for growth.

However, Berlin criticizes the dangers of this view. By assuming that others know what is best for individuals, he can justify coercion in the name of "true freedom." This notion extends to collective entities such as states or nations, where individual autonomy is often sacrificed for the sake of collective goals. Berlin warns that while self-realization offers an inspiring vision of human potential, it risks becoming a tool for authoritarianism, undermining authentic personal freedom.

Sarastro's temple

In Sarastro's Temple, Isaiah Berlin explores how the pursuit of rational self-direction, fundamental to positive freedom, can lead to authoritarianism when applied to society. Rationalist thinkers such as Rousseau and Kant envisioned a society in which laws align with the rational will of individuals, making obedience to those laws a form of freedom. In this idealized vision, a rational state governs by laws that all rational individuals would voluntarily accept, harmonizing individual and collective interests. However, Berlin criticizes the assumption that rationality always leads to universal agreement, warning that this belief often results in the imposition of laws by an elite who claim to know the "true" will of the people.

This rationalist framework, Berlin argues, can justify coercion under the guise of liberation. Leaders or ideologues can repress dissent and impose their vision of a rational order, insisting that those who resist are irrational or wrong. This transforms positive freedom into a tool of control, equating freedom with submission to authority. Berlin highlights the danger of confusing individual and collective wills, where the "real self" becomes a justification for overriding real individual desires. The chapter underscores Berlin's concern that philosophical ideals of rational self-government may, in practice, lead to the suppression of freedom in the name of a supposed higher good.

The search for status

In The Search for Status, Isaiah Berlin examines how the human desire for recognition and dignity is intertwined with the concept of freedom. Beyond seeking freedom from interference or the capacity for self-direction, individuals and groups often yearn for recognition of their uniqueness and value within society. Berlin argues that this quest for status is essential to personal identity, as individuals define themselves in part through how others perceive them. This dynamic extends to groups, such as nations or classes, who seek collective recognition of their cultural, social or political importance. For many, being treated as equals in dignity and status is as vital as legal rights or personal autonomy.

Berlin highlights how this desire for recognition can sometimes conflict with the pursuit of freedom. Groups may prioritize the assertion of their status over the preservation of individual freedoms, leading them to prefer to be governed by members of their own community, however authoritarian, rather than by outsiders perceived as indifferent or condescending. Although this yearning for status fosters solidarity and dignity, Berlin warns against confusing it with freedom itself. Recognition is a distinct human need that complements, but does not replace, the essence of freedom. In clarifying this distinction, Berlin underscores the complexity of human aspirations and the challenges of balancing freedom with the deep need for social recognition.

Freedom and sovereignty

In the chapter on Freedom and Sovereignty, Isaiah Berlin explores the tension between individual freedom and the collective authority represented by sovereignty. He highlights the distinction between negative freedom, which emphasizes freedom from interference, and positive freedom, which focuses on self-mastery and participation in collective government. The notion of sovereignty often coincides with that of positive freedom, as it suggests that individuals achieve freedom by participating in the decisions that govern their lives. However, Berlin warns that this merger can lead to the subjugation of individual liberties to collective authority, as sovereignty often manifests itself as the will of a majority or elite group imposing its vision on others.

Berlin criticizes the assumption that collective decisions inherently preserve individual freedom. He argues that the questions of "who governs me" and "to what extent does the government interfere with me" are distinct. A democratic society may curtail individual liberties in the name of collective goals, while an autocracy may allow significant personal autonomy in private life. Berlin stresses that sovereignty, when unchecked, can become a tool of coercion under the guise of rational government or the general will. By confusing freedom with sovereignty, societies risk undermining the very freedom they seek to protect, as individuals are subordinated to collective goals that may not coincide with their autonomy or personal desires.

The one and the multitude

In The One and the Multitude, Isaiah Berlin examines the inherent conflict between the quest for universal ideals and the pluralistic nature of human values. He argues that belief in a single ultimate truth or ideal-the hallmark of many philosophical and political systems-often clashes with the reality that human beings have diverse, sometimes incompatible, values and aspirations. Berlin criticizes the assumption that all legitimate human goals can be harmonized into a single, coherent system, claiming that this belief ignores the complexity of human experience and leads to oversimplification. He stresses that the richness of human life lies in its diversity, and that attempts to impose a universal framework often suppress this plurality in favor of rigid conformity.

It also warns us of the dangers of monistic systems that seek to reconcile all values into an overarching ideal, whether rooted in religion, ideology or reason. These systems tend to marginalize or eliminate values and ways of life that do not fit into their framework, often in the name of progress or rationality. The pursuit of "the one" undermines the legitimacy of "the multiple," as it sacrifices individual freedom and diversity for the sake of an illusory unity.

Berlin advocates a pluralistic approach that recognizes the coexistence of competing values and the need for compromise, acknowledging that this tension is an inevitable and valuable part of the human condition.

By embracing diversity, societies can better protect individual freedoms and resist authoritarian impulses that arise from a belief in a singular truth.

TWO CONCEPTS OF LIBERTY

Introduction

To coerce a man is to deprive him of his freedom.

Freedom from what?

Almost every moralist in human history has praised freedom.

Like happiness and goodness, like nature and reality, the meaning of this term is so porous that there are few interpretations it seems able to resist.

I do not propose to discuss either the history or the more than two hundred meanings of this protean word, recorded by historians of ideas. I propose to examine no more than two of these meanings, but the central ones, with a great deal of human history behind them and, I dare say, still to come.

The first of these political senses of freedom, which I will call the "negative" sense, is implicit in the answer to the question "What is the area within which the subject-a person or group of persons-can or should be able to do or be what he or she is capable of doing or being, without interference from other persons?

The second, which I will call positive sense, is involved in the answer to the question "What or who is the source of control or interference that can determine someone to do or be one thing rather than another?".

The two questions are clearly different, although their answers may coincide.

The idea of "negative" freedom

It is usually said that I am free to the extent that no human being interferes with my activity. In this sense, political freedom is simply the sphere in which a man can act without being hindered by others. If other people prevent me from doing what I could otherwise do, to that degree I am not free; and if this area is restricted by other men beyond a certain minimum, I may be said to be coerced or, perhaps, enslaved.

However, coercion is not a term that encompasses all forms of incapacity. If I say that I am unable to jump more than ten feet in the air, or that I cannot read because I am blind, or that I cannot understand the more obscure pages of Hegel, it would be eccentric to say that I am to that degree enslaved or coerced. Coercion involves the deliberate interference of other human beings in the realm in which I might otherwise act. Political freedom is only lacking if human beings prevent the attainment of a goal.

The mere inability to achieve an objective is not a lack of political freedom. This is evidenced by the use of such modern expressions as "economic freedom" and its counterpart, "economic slavery."

It is argued, quite plausibly, that if a man is too poor to afford something that is not forbidden by law-a loaf of bread, a trip around the world, recourse to the courts-he is as unfree to have it as he would be if forbidden by the Law.

If my poverty were a kind of disease that prevented me from buying bread or paying for the trip around the world, or getting my case heard, as lameness prevents me from running, this inability would not naturally be described as a lack of freedom, still less of political freedom. It is only because I believe that my inability to get a certain thing is due to the fact that other human beings have made arrangements whereby I - while others do not - am prevented from having enough money with which to pay for it, that I consider myself a victim of coercion or slavery.

In other words, this use of the term depends on a certain social and economic theory about the causes of my poverty or weakness. If my lack of material means is due to my lack of mental or physical capacity, then I begin to speak of being deprived of liberty (and not simply of poverty) only if I accept this theory. If, in addition, I believe that I am kept in misery by a specific arrangement that I consider unjust or inequitable, I speak of economic slavery or oppression.

"The nature of things does not drive us mad, only ill will does," said Rousseau.

The criterion of oppression is the role I believe other human beings play, directly or indirectly, intentionally or unintentionally, in frustrating my desires. By being free in this sense I mean not being interfered with by others. The wider the zone of non-interference, the wider my freedom. This is what classical English philosophers and politicians meant when they used this word. Although they did not agree on how wide that zone could or should be.

They supposed that, as things stood, it could not be unlimited, for if it were, it would imply a state in which all men could interfere unlimitedly with all other men; and this kind of "natural" liberty would lead to social chaos in which the minimum needs of men would not be satisfied; or else the liberties of the weak would be suppressed by the strong. Because they perceived that human ends and activities do not automatically harmonize with each other; and, because (whatever their official doctrines) they placed great value on other goals, such as justice, or happiness, or culture, or security, or various degrees of equality.

They were willing to restrict freedom in the interest of other values and, indeed, of freedom itself. For, without it, it was impossible to create the kind of association they considered desirable.

Consequently, these thinkers assumed that the scope of men's free action must be limited by law. But it is also assumed-especially by libertarians such as Locke and Mill in England, and Constant and

Tocqueville in France-that there must be a certain minimum area of personal freedom which must not be violated on any account; for if it is exceeded, the individual will find himself in an area too narrow even for that minimum development of his natural faculties which alone makes it possible to pursue-and even to conceive-of the various ends which men consider good or right or sacred.

It follows that a boundary must be drawn between the realm of private life and that of public authority. Where it should be drawn is a matter of discussion, even haggling.

Men are largely interdependent, and no one man's activity is so completely private as not to impede in any way the lives of others. "Liberty to the pike is death to the minnow"; the freedom of some must depend upon the restraint of others.

Still, a practical compromise must be found. Philosophers who took an optimistic view of human nature and believed in the possibility of harmonizing human interests, such as Locke or Adam Smith and, at times, Mill, believed that social harmony and progress were compatible with the reservation of ample space for private life, into which neither the state nor any other authority should encroach.

Hobbes, and those who agreed with him, especially conservative or reactionary thinkers, held that if men were to be prevented from destroying one another and turning social life into a jungle or a wilderness, greater safeguards must be instituted to keep them in their places, and they wished, accordingly, to increase the area of centralized control and diminish that of the individual.

But both sides agreed that a part of human existence should remain independent of the sphere of social control. To encroach on that preserve, however small, would be despotism.

The most eloquent of all the defenders of liberty and privacy, Benjamin Constant, who had not forgotten the Jacobin dictatorship, declared that, at the very least, freedom of religion, opinion, speech and property must be guaranteed against arbitrary invasion. Jefferson, Burke, Paine, Mill, compiled different catalogs of individual liberties, but the argument for keeping authority at bay is always substantially the same:

We must preserve a minimum space of personal freedom if we do not want to "degrade or deny our nature". We cannot remain absolutely free, and we must give up part of our freedom to preserve the rest. But total surrender is counterproductive.

What then must be the minimum: that which man cannot give up without infringing on the essence of his human nature? What is this essence? What are the norms it implies? This has been, and perhaps always will be, the subject of endless debates. But whatever the principle according to which the zone of non-interference is delimited, whether it be that of natural law or that of natural rights, or that of utility or that of the pronouncements of a categorical imperative, or that of the sanctity of the social contract, or any other concept by which men have sought to clarify and justify their convictions, freedom in this sense means "freedom from." It means absence of interference beyond the shifting but always recognizable boundary.

"The only freedom that deserves that name is the freedom to pursue our own good in our own way," said the most celebrated of its advocates. If this is so, is coercion ever justified?

Mill had no doubt that it was. Since justice demands that all individuals be entitled to a minimum of liberty, all other individuals must necessarily be restrained, if necessary by force, from depriving anyone of it.

In fact, the whole function of the law was the prevention of such collisions: the state was reduced to what Lassalle disparagingly described as the functions of a night watchman or a traffic policeman.

What made the protection of individual liberty so sacred to Mill? In his famous essay he declares that unless men are left to live as they will "in the way that concerns themselves alone," civilization cannot advance; truth will not come to light in the absence of a free market of ideas; there will be no room for spontaneity, originality, genius, for mental energy, for moral courage... Society will be crushed by the weight of "collective mediocrity." All that is rich and diversified will be crushed by the weight of habit, by the constant tendency of men to conformity, which only engenders "withered capacities", human beings "reduced and corseted", "shrunken and deformed". "Pagan self-assertion is as worthy as Christian self-denial."

All the mistakes a man can make against advice and warnings are far outweighed by the evil of allowing others to force him to do what they consider good. The defense of freedom consists in the "negative" goal of avoiding interference.

To threaten a man with persecution if he does not submit to a life in which he cannot choose his goals; to bar before him all but one door, however noble the prospect that opens or however benevolent the motives of those who open it, is to sin against the truth that he is a man, a being with a life of his own to live. This is freedom as conceived by the liberals of the modern world from the time of Erasmus (some would say Occam) to our own.

Every plea for civil liberties and individual rights, every protest against exploitation and humiliation, against the encroachment of public authority, or the mass hypnosis of custom or organized propaganda, springs from this individualistic, and much disputed, conception of man.

Three facts about this position are worth noting:

First, Mill confuses two distinct notions. One is that all coercion is, insofar as it frustrates human desires, bad as such, even if it has to be applied to prevent other, greater evils; while non-interference, which is the opposite of coercion, is good as such, even if it is not the only good. This is the "negative" conception of freedom in its classical form.

The other is that men should try to discover truth, or to develop a certain kind of character that Mill approves of - fearless, original, imaginative, independent, nonconformist to the point of eccentricity, etc. - and that truth can be found, and such a character can be bred, only under conditions of freedom.

Both are liberal views, but they are not identical, and the connection between them is at best empirical.

No one would say that truth or freedom of speech can flourish where dogma crushes all thought. But the evidence of history tends to show (as, indeed, James Stephen argued in his formidable attack on Mill in his Liberty, Equality, Fraternity) that integrity, love of truth, and ardent individualism grow at least as often in severely disciplined communities-among, for example, Puritan Calvinists in Scotland or New England, or under military discipline-as in more tolerant or indifferent societies, and if this is so accepted, Mill's argument for liberty as a necessary condition for the growth of human genius collapses.

If his two goals proved incompatible, Mill would face a cruel dilemma, apart from the additional difficulties created by the inconsistency of his doctrines with strict utilitarianism, even in his own human version of it.

Secondly, the doctrine is comparatively modern. It seems that in the ancient world there was hardly any talk of individual liberty as a conscious political ideal (as opposed to its actual existence).

Condorcet has already pointed out that the notion of individual rights is absent from the juridical conceptions of the Romans and the Greeks; the same seems to be true of the Jews, the Chinese, and all other ancient civilizations that have come to light since.

The dominance of this ideal has been the exception rather than the rule, even in the recent history of the West.

Nor has freedom in this sense often constituted a rallying cry for the great masses of mankind. The desire not to be disturbed, to be left to one's own devices, has been a mark of high civilization on the part of both individuals and communities.

The sense of privacy itself, of the realm of personal relationships as sacred in its own right, derives from a conception of freedom which, for all its religious roots, is hardly older, in its developed state, than the Renaissance or the Reformation. Yet its decline would mark the death of a civilization, of an entire moral outlook.

The third characteristic of this notion of freedom is of greater importance. It is that freedom in this sense is not incompatible with some types of autocracy, or at any rate with the absence of self-government.

Freedom in this sense has to do primarily with the area of control, not with its source.

Just as a democracy may, in fact, deprive the individual citizen of many liberties he might have in some other form of society, it is perfectly conceivable that a liberal-minded despot would allow his subjects a large measure of personal freedom. The despot who allows his subjects a large measure of liberty may be unjust, or encourage the wildest inequalities, care little for order, or virtue, or knowledge, but so long as he does not abridge their liberty, or at least abridge it less than many other regimes, he meets Mill's specification.

Freedom in this sense is in any case not logically related to democracy or self-government. Self-government may, in general, provide a better guarantee of the preservation of civil liberties than other regimes, and has been advocated as such by libertarians. But there is no necessary connection between individual liberty and democratic government.

The answer to the question "who governs me?" is logically different from the question "to what extent does government interfere with me?"

It is in this difference that the great contrast between the two concepts of negative and positive freedom ultimately consists. For the "positive" sense of freedom comes to light if we try to answer the question, not "what am I free to do or be?", but "who governs me?" or "who says what I should or should not be or do?".

The connection between democracy and individual liberty is much more tenuous than it seemed to many advocates of both. The desire to be governed by myself, or at any rate to participate in the process by which my life is to be controlled, may be as deep a desire as that for a free space for action, and perhaps historically older. But it is not the same desire. In fact, it is so different that it has ultimately led to the great clash of ideologies that dominates our world.

For it is this-the "positive" conception of freedom: not "freedom from," but "freedom to"-that the proponents of the "negative" idea of freedom portray as something that is sometimes no more than a deceptive disguise for brutal tyranny.

The idea of positive freedom

The "positive" meaning of the word "freedom" derives from the individual's desire to be his own master.

"I wish my life and my decisions to depend on myself, not on external forces of any kind. I desire to be the instrument of my own acts of will, not those of others. I wish to be a subject, not an object; to be moved by reasons, by conscious purposes that are mine, not by causes that affect me, as it were, from without. I wish to be somebody, not nobody; a doer - deciding, not being decided, self-directed and not acted upon by external nature or by other men as if I were a thing, or an animal, or a slave incapable of playing a human role, that is, of conceiving aims and policies of my own and realizing them." "This is at least part of what I mean when I assert that I am rational, and that it is my reason that distinguishes me as a human being from the rest of the world. I wish, above all, to be conscious of myself as a thinking, willful, active being, responsible for his choices and capable of explaining them by reference to his own ideas and purposes." "I feel free insofar as I believe this to be true, and enslaved insofar as I am made to see that it is not."

The freedom that consists in owning oneself and the freedom that consists in not being prevented by others from choosing as I do may seem, at first glance, to be concepts that are not logically very far apart from each other; they are but negative and positive ways of saying the same thing. However, the "positive" and "negative" notions of freedom developed historically in divergent directions, not always by logically accredited steps, until, in the end, they came into direct conflict with each other.

One way of bringing this out is the independent momentum that the metaphor of self-mastery, at first perhaps quite harmless, acquired. "I am my own master"; "I am no one's slave"; but can I not (as, for example, T. H. Green always says) be the slave of nature? Or of my own "unbridled" passions? Have men not had the experience of freeing themselves from spiritual slavery, or from the slavery of nature, and have they not in the course of it become aware, on the one hand, of a dominating self and, on the other, of something in them that is subdued?

This dominant self is then identified in various ways with reason, with my "higher nature", with the self that calculates and seeks what will satisfy it in the long run, with my "real", or "ideal", or "autonomous" self, or with my self "at its best"; which is opposed to the irrational impulse, to uncontrolled desires, to my "lower" nature, to the pursuit of immediate pleasures, to my "empirical" or "heteronomous" self, swept along by every burst of desire and passion, which needs to be rigidly disciplined if it is ever to rise to the full height of its "real" nature.

In actuality, the two selves can be represented as divided by an even greater gap: the real self can be conceived of as something broader than the individual (as this term is normally understood), as a social "whole" of which the individual is an element or aspect: a tribe, a race, a church, a state, the great society of the living and the dead and the unborn. This entity is then identified as the "true" self which, by imposing its unique collective or "organic" will on its recalcitrant "members," achieves its own freedom and thus theirs. A "superior" will.

The dangers of using organic metaphors to justify the coercion of some men by others in order to raise them to a "higher" level of freedom have often been pointed out. But what gives such plausibility to this kind of language is that we recognize that it is possible, and sometimes justifiable, to coerce men in the name of some goal (say, justice or public health) that they themselves would pursue if they were more enlightened, but do not do so because they are blind or ignorant or corrupt.

This makes it easy for me to conceive of myself coercing others for their own sake, in their interest, not mine. I then assert that I know what they really need better than they themselves do.

What, at best, this implies is that they would not resist me if they were rational and as wise as I am, and understood their interests as I do. But I can state much more than that. I can declare that, in reality, they aspire to that which, in their state of ignorance, they consciously resist, because there exists within them a hidden entity-their latent rational will, or their "true" purpose-and that this entity, though belied by all that they openly feel, do, and say, is their "real" self, of which the poor empirical self in space and time may know nothing or very little; and that this inner spirit is the only self that deserves to have its wishes taken into account.

Having adopted this point of view, I am in a position to ignore the real desires of men or societies, to bully them, oppress them, torture them in the name and on account of their "true" self, in the certainty that whatever the real aim of man (happiness, the fulfillment of duty, wisdom, a just society, self-realization) must be identical with his freedom, the free choice of his "true" self, though submerged and inarticulate.

This paradox has often been exposed. It is one thing to say that I know what is good for X, while he himself does not, and even to ignore his desires for his sake; and quite another to say that he has chosen it for himself, not consciously, not as it appears in everyday life, but in his role as a rational self that his empirical self may not know, the "real" self that discerns the good and cannot help but choose it once it reveals itself.

This monstrous impersonation, which consists in equating what X would choose if it were something it is not, or at least not yet, with what X actually seeks and chooses, is at the heart of all political theories of self-realization. It is one thing to say that I can be coerced for my own good, that I am too blind to see: this may, on occasion, be to my benefit; indeed, it may enlarge the scope of my freedom; it is another thing to say that it suits my good, then I am not being coerced, because I have willed it, whether I know it or not, and I am free - or "truly" free - even while my poor earthly body and foolish mind bitterly reject it, and fight against those who seek, however benevolently, to impose it, with the utmost desperation.

This magical transformation, or sleight of hand (for which William James so justly derided the Hegelians), can no doubt be perpetrated just as easily with the "negative" concept of freedom, where the self with which one must not interfere is no longer the individual with his real desires and needs as normally conceived, but the "real" man within, identified with the pursuit of some ideal purpose undreamed of by his empirical self. And, as in the case of the "positively" free self, this entity may be contained in some superpersonal entity - a state, a class, a nation, or the march of history itself, regarded as a subject of more "real" attributes than the empirical self.

But the "positive" conception of freedom as self-mastery, with its suggestion of a man divided against himself, has, in fact, and as a matter of the history of doctrines and practice, lent itself more readily to this division of personality into two: the transcendent and dominant controller, and the empirical bundle of desires and passions to be disciplined and mastered. This demonstrates (if such an obvious truth needs to be demonstrated) that the conception of freedom derives directly from one's view of what constitutes a self, a person, a man. It is enough to manipulate the definition of man for freedom to acquire whatever meaning the manipulator wishes. Recent history has made it abundantly clear that the question is not merely academic.

The consequences of the distinction between two selves will become even clearer if one considers the two main forms that the desire for self-direction -directed by the "true" self-has historically taken: the first, that of self-abnegation to achieve independence; the second, that of self-realization, or total self-identification with a specific principle or ideal to achieve the same end.

Retreat to the inner citadel

I am possessed of reason and will; I conceive ends and desire to pursue them; but if I am prevented from achieving them I no longer feel in control of the situation.

I may be prevented by the laws of nature, or by accidents, or by the activities of men, or by the often undesigned effect of human institutions. These forces may be too much for me.

What must I do not to be crushed by them? I must free myself from desires that I know I cannot fulfill.

I desire to be master of my realm, but my boundaries are long and insecure, so I contract them to reduce or eliminate the vulnerable zone.

I begin by desiring happiness, or power, or knowledge, or the attainment of some particular object. But I cannot command them. Thus, I choose to avoid defeat and waste, and therefore decide not to strive for anything I cannot be sure of obtaining.

I choose not to desire what is unattainable.

The tyrant threatens me with the destruction of my property, with imprisonment, with exile or the death of my loved ones. But if I no longer feel attached to property, if I no longer care whether or not I am in prison, if I have killed within me my natural affections, then he cannot bend me to his will, because all that remains of me is no longer subject to empirical fears or desires. It is as if I have strategically withdrawn into an inner citadel-my reason, my soul, my "noumenal" self-that, whatever they do, neither blind outside force, nor human malice, can touch.

I have shut myself up within myself; there, and there alone, I am safe. It is as if I were to say, "I have a wound in my leg." There are two methods to free me from pain. One is to heal the wound. But if healing is too difficult or uncertain, there is another method. I can get rid of the wound by cutting off my leg. If I train myself not to desire anything for which the possession of my leg is indispensable, I will not feel the lack of it."

It is the traditional self-emancipation of ascetics and quietists, of Stoics or Buddhist sages, of men of various religions or none at all, who have fled the world and escaped the yoke of society or public opinion by some process of deliberate self-transformation that allows them to no longer care about any of their values, to remain, isolated and independent, within their borders, no longer vulnerable to weapons.

All political isolationism, all economic autarky, all forms of autonomy, have in them some element of this attitude.

I remove the obstacles in my way by abandoning the road; I retreat into my own sect, into my own planned economy, into my own deliberately isolated territory, where no voices from outside need be heard, and where no external force can have any effect. This is a form of the search for security; but it has also been called the search for personal or national freedom or independence.

From this doctrine, as applied to individuals, there is not much distance to the conceptions of those who, like Kant, identify freedom no longer with the elimination of desires, but with resistance to them and control over them.

"I identify myself with the controller and escape the bondage of the controlled. I am free because, and insofar as, I am autonomous. I obey the laws, but I have imposed them on myself or found them in my own uncoerced self."

Freedom is obedience, but, in Rousseau's words, "obedience to a law which we prescribe to ourselves," and no man can enslave himself.

Heteronomy is dependence on external factors, the responsibility of being a plaything of the external world which I myself cannot fully control, and which therefore controls and "enslaves" me.

I am only free insofar as my person is not "chained" to anything that obeys forces over which I have no control; I cannot control the laws of nature; therefore, my free activity must rise above the empirical world of causality.

This is not the place to discuss the validity of this ancient and famous doctrine; I only wish to point out that related notions of freedom as "resistance to" (or "escape from") an unrealizable desire, and as independence from the sphere of causality, have played a central role in politics no less than in ethics.

For if the essence of men is that they are autonomous beings-authors of values, of ends in themselves, whose ultimate authority consists precisely in their being freely willed-then nothing is worse than to treat them as if they were not autonomous, but natural objects, played by causal influences, creatures at the mercy of external stimuli, whose choices can be manipulated by their rulers, whether by threats of force or offers of rewards. To treat men in this way is to treat them as if they were not self-determined.

"No one can force me to be happy in his own way," said Kant. Paternalism is "the greatest despotism imaginable."

This is so because it is to treat men as if they were not free, but human material for me, the benevolent reformer, to mold according to my own freely adopted purpose, not theirs.

This is, of course, precisely the policy recommended by the early utilitarians. Helvetius (and Bentham) did not believe in resisting, but in utilizing, the tendency of men to be slaves to their passions; they wished to dangle rewards and punishments before men-the sharpest possible form of heteronomy-if by this means the "slaves" could be happier. But to manipulate men, to drive them toward goals that you - the social reformer - see, but they cannot see, is to deny their human essence, to treat them as objects without a will of their own, and thus to degrade them. Therefore, to lie to men or to deceive them, that is, to use them as means to my ends, not theirs, independently conceived, even if for their own benefit, is, in effect, to treat them as subhuman, to behave as if their ends were less ultimate and sacred than mine.

In the name of what can I justify forcing men to do what they have not wanted or consented to? Only in the name of some value higher than themselves. But if, as Kant held, all values are made so by the free acts of men, and called values only in so far as they are this, there is no value superior to the individual. To do this, therefore, is to coerce men in the name of something less ultimate than themselves: to bend them to my will, or to another person's particular craving for (his) happiness or comfort or safety or convenience.

"My aim is something desired (for whatever reason, however noble) by myself or my group, for which I use other men as means."

But this is a contradiction to what men are, i.e., ends in themselves. All ways of manipulating human beings, of reaching out to them, of molding them against their will according to your own pattern, all thought control and conditioning, is thus a denial of that in men which makes them men and their ultimate values.

Kant's free individual is a transcendent being, beyond the realm of natural causality. But in its empirical form - in which the notion of man is that of ordinary life - this doctrine was at the heart of liberal humanism, both moral and political, which was deeply influenced by both Kant and Rousseau in the eighteenth century.

In its a priori version, it is a form of secularized Protestant individualism, in which the place of God is taken by the conception of rational life, and the place of the individual soul striving to unite with Him is replaced by the conception of the individual, endowed with reason, striving to be governed by reason and reason alone, and not to be dependent on anything that might lead him astray or mislead him by compromising his irrational nature.

Autonomy, not heteronomy: to act and not to be acted upon.

The notion of slavery to the passions is - for those who think in these terms - something more than a metaphor. To free myself from fear, or from love, or from the desire to conform, is to free myself from the despotism of something I cannot control.

Sophocles, of whom Plato says that only old age has freed him from the passion of love-the yoke of a cruel master-is relating an experience as real as that of liberation from a human tyrant or a slaveholder.

The psychological experience of observing myself yielding to some "lower" impulse, acting from a motive I dislike, or of doing something which at the very moment of doing it I may detest, and reflecting later that "I was not myself," or "not in control of myself," when I did it, belongs to this way of thinking and speaking.

"I identify with my critical and rational moments. The consequences of my actions cannot matter, because they are not under my control; only my motives are."

This is the creed of the solitary thinker who has defied the world and emancipated himself from the fetters of men and things.

In this form, the doctrine may seem primarily an ethical creed, and scarcely a political one; however, its political implications are clear, and it enters into the tradition of liberal individualism at least as deeply as the "negative" concept of freedom.

It is perhaps worth noting that, in its individualistic form, the concept of the rational sage who has escaped the inner fortress of his true self seems to emerge when the outer world has proved exceptionally arid, cruel, or unjust.

"He is truly free," said Rousseau, "who desires what he can accomplish and does what he wishes."

In a world where a man seeking happiness, justice or freedom (in any sense) can do little, because he finds too many avenues of action blocked, the temptation to withdraw into himself can become irresistible.

It may have been so in Greece, where the Stoic ideal cannot be entirely unrelated to the fall of the independent democracies before the centralized Macedonian autocracy. It was so in Rome, for analogous reasons, after the end of the Republic. It arose in

Germany in the seventeenth century, during the period of the greatest national degradation of the German states following the Thirty Years' War, when the character of public life, particularly in the small principalities, forced those who cherished the dignity of human life, not for the first and not for the last time, into a kind of inward emigration.

The doctrine that what I cannot have I must teach myself not to desire, that a desire removed, or successfully resisted, is as good as a desire satisfied is a sublime, but, it seems to me, unmistakable, form of the sour grapes doctrine: what I cannot be sure of, I cannot truly want.

This makes it clear why the definition of negative freedom as the ability to do what one wishes-which is, in effect, the definition adopted by Mill-is of no avail.

If I find that I can do little or nothing of what I desire, I need only contract or extinguish my desires, and I am already free.

If the tyrant (or "hidden persuader") succeeds in conditioning his subjects (or clients) to lose their original desires and adopt ("internalize") the way of life he has invented for them, he will have succeeded, according to this definition, in freeing them.

No doubt he will have made them feel free, as Epictetus feels freer than his master (and it is said that the proverbial good man feels happy on the rack). But what he has created is the very antithesis of political freedom. Ascetic self-denial may be a source of integrity or serenity and spiritual strength, but it is hard to see how it can be called an extension of freedom.

If I save myself from an adversary by retreating inward and locking all entrances and exits, I may still be freer than if I had been captured by him, but am I freer than if I had defeated or captured him? If I go too far, if I contract into too small a space, I will suffocate and die.

The logical culmination of the process of destroying everything by which I can be hurt is suicide. As long as I exist in the natural world, I can never be totally secure. Total liberation in this sense (as Schopenhauer correctly perceived) is conferred only by death.

I live in a world in which I encounter obstacles to my will. Perhaps those who cling to the "negative" concept of freedom can be forgiven if they think that self-denial is not the only method of overcoming obstacles; that it is also possible to do so by removing them: in the case of non-human objects, by physical action; in the case of human resistance, by force or persuasion, as when I induce someone to make room for me in his carriage, or conquer a country that threatens the interests of my own.

Such acts may be unjust, they may involve violence, cruelty, the enslavement of others, but it can hardly be denied that by so doing the agent is able, in the most literal sense, to increase his own freedom.

It is an irony of history that this truth is repudiated by some of those who practice it most forcibly, men who, even as they conquer power and freedom of action, reject the "negative" concept of it in favor of its "positive" counterpart. Their point of view dominates half of our world; let us see on what metaphysical foundation it rests.

Self-realization

We are told that the only true method of attaining freedom is the use of critical reason, the understanding of what is necessary and what is contingent.

If I am a schoolboy, all but the simplest mathematical truths present themselves as obstacles to the free functioning of my mind, as theorems whose necessity I do not understand; some external authority declares them to be true and they present themselves to me as foreign bodies which I am expected to absorb mechanically into my system. But when I understand the functions of the symbols, the axioms, the rules of formation and transformation-the logic by which conclusions are obtained-and understand that these things cannot be otherwise, because they seem to follow from the laws governing the processes of my own reason, then mathematical truths no longer impose themselves as external entities forced upon me which I must receive whether I want them or not, but as something I now freely will in the course of the natural functioning of my own rational activity.

For the mathematician, the proof of these theorems is part of the free exercise of his natural reasoning ability. For the musician, once he has assimilated the composer's pattern of the score and made the composer's aims his own, the performance of music is not obedience to external laws, a compulsion and a barrier to freedom, but a free and unfettered exercise.

The interpreter is not tied to the score as the ox to the plow or the worker to the machine. He has absorbed the score into his own system, by understanding it, he has identified it with himself, it has passed from being an impediment to free activity to being an element of the activity itself.

What applies to music or mathematics must, we are told, apply in principle to all other obstacles which present themselves as so many lumps of external matter blocking free self-development.

That is the program of enlightened rationalism from Spinoza to the later (sometimes unconscious) disciples of Hegel. "Sapere aude." What you know, that of which you understand the necessity - the rational necessity - you cannot, without ceasing to be rational, want it to be otherwise. For to want something to be otherwise than it ought to be is, given the premises - the necessities that govern the world - to be therefore either ignorant or irrational.

Passions, prejudices, fears, neuroses arise from ignorance and take the form of myths and illusions.

To be dominated by myths, whether they come from the imagination of unscrupulous charlatans who deceive us in order to exploit us, or from psychological or sociological causes, is a form of heteronomy, of being dominated by external factors in a direction not necessarily desired by the agent.

The scientific determinists of the eighteenth century supposed that the study of the sciences of nature, and the creation of sciences of society on the same model, would make transparently clear the workings of such causes, and thus enable individuals to recognize their own part, in the workings of a rational world, frustrating only when misunderstood.

Knowledge liberates, as Epicurus taught long ago, automatically eliminating irrational fears and desires.

Herder, Hegel and Marx replaced the old mechanical models with their own vitalistic models of social life, but they believed, like their opponents, that to understand the world is to liberate.

They differed from them only in stressing the role of change and growth in what makes human beings human.

Social life cannot be understood by analogy with mathematics or physics. One must also understand history, that is, the peculiar laws of continuous growth, whether by dialectical conflict or otherwise, that govern individuals and groups in their interaction with each other and with nature. Not to understand this is, according to these thinkers, to fall into a particular kind of error, namely, the belief that human nature is static, that its essential properties are the same everywhere and at all times, that it is governed by unchanging natural laws, whether conceived in theological or materialistic terms, which leads to the fallacious corollary that a wise legislator can, in principle, create a perfectly harmonious society at any time by appropriate education and legislation, because rational men, in all ages and countries, must always demand the same unchanging satisfactions of the same unchanging basic needs.

Hegel believed that his contemporaries (and indeed all his predecessors) misunderstood the nature of institutions because they did not understand the laws - the rationally intelligible laws, since they arise from the operation of reason - that create and alter institutions and transform human character and human action.

Marx and his disciples argued that the path of human beings was hindered not only by natural forces or the imperfections of their own character, but, even more, by the operation of their own social institutions, which they had originally created (not always consciously) for certain ends, but whose operation they came to systematically misunderstand, and which then became obstacles to the progress of their creators.

Marx offered social and economic hypotheses to explain the inevitability of such misunderstanding, in particular of the illusion that such man-made arrangements were independent forces, as inescapable as the laws of nature. As examples of such pseudo-objective forces, he pointed to the laws of supply and demand, or the institution of property, or the eternal division of society into rich and poor, or owners and workers, as so many other unchanging human categories.

Only when we had reached a stage where the spells of these illusions could be broken, that is, until a sufficient number of men reached a social stage which would enable them to understand that these laws and institutions were themselves the work of human minds and hands, historically necessary in their time, and later confounded with inexorable and objective powers, could the old world be destroyed and replaced by a more adequate and liberating social machinery.

"We are enslaved by despots-institutions or beliefs or neuroses-which can only be removed by analysis and understanding. We are prisoners of evil spirits which we ourselves - though not consciously - have created, and we can only exorcise them by becoming aware and acting appropriately." Indeed, for Marx, understanding is proper action.

I am free if, and only if, I plan my life according to my own will; plans imply rules; a rule neither oppresses nor enslaves me if I consciously impose it on myself, or freely accept it, having understood it, whether invented by me or by others, provided it is rational, that is, in accordance with the necessities of things. To understand why things should be as they should be is to want them to be so.

Knowledge liberates not by offering us more open possibilities from which to choose, but by preserving us from the frustration of attempting the impossible.

To want the necessary laws to be other than what they are is to fall prey to an irrational desire: the desire that what must be X should also be non-X. To go beyond that, and to believe that these laws are other than what they necessarily are, is to be insane.

That is the metaphysical heart of rationalism. The notion of freedom it contains is not the "negative" conception of an (ideally) unobstructed field, a vacuum in which nothing obstructs me, but the notion of self-direction or self-control.

"I can do whatever I want with my own. I am a rational being; whatever I can demonstrate to myself as necessary, as incapable of being otherwise in a rational society - that is, in a society directed by rational minds, toward goals such as a rational being would have - I cannot, being rational, wish to sweep out of my way." "I assimilate it to my substance as I do the laws of logic, of mathematics, from which I can never be thwarted, since I cannot wish it to be other than what it is."

This is the positive doctrine of liberation by reason. Its socialized forms, so disparate and opposed to each other, constitute the core of many of the nationalist, communist, authoritarian and totalitarian creeds of our day.

It is possible that, in the course of its evolution, it has strayed far from its rationalist roots. Nevertheless, it is this freedom that, in democracies and dictatorships, is discussed and fought for today in many parts of the world.

Without pretending to trace the historical evolution of this idea, I would like to comment on some of its vicissitudes:

Temple of Sarastro

Those who believed in freedom as rational self-direction were forced, sooner or later, to consider how it should apply not only to man's inner life, but also to his relations with other members of society. Even the most individualistic - Rousseau, Kant, and Fichte certainly began as individualists - came at some point to ask whether a rational life was possible not only for the individual, but also for society, and if so, how it was to be achieved.

"I wish to be free to live as my rational will (my "real self") commands, but so must others. How am I to avoid clashing with their wills? Where is the boundary between my (rationally determined) rights and the identical rights of others? For if I am rational, I cannot deny that what is right for me must be right, for the same reasons, for others who are rational like me."

A rational (or free) state would be a state governed by laws that all rational men would freely accept; that is, laws that they themselves would have enacted if they had been asked what, as rational beings, they demanded; therefore, the boundaries would be what all rational men would consider the right boundaries for rational beings.

But, in reality, who was to determine what those boundaries were?

Thinkers of this type held that if moral and political problems were genuine-as they undoubtedly were-they must in principle be soluble; that is, there must be one and only one true solution to any problem. All truths could be discovered in principle by any rational thinker, and demonstrated so clearly that all other rational men could not but accept them; indeed, this was already largely the case in the new natural sciences.

On this assumption, the problem of political freedom was solved by establishing a just order that would give each man all the freedom to which a rational being is entitled.

My claim to unrestricted freedom may, at first sight, sometimes not be reconciled with the equally unrestricted claim of another person; but the rational solution of one problem cannot collide with the equally true solution of another, for two truths cannot be logically incompatible; therefore, in principle it must be possible to discover a just order, an order whose rules make possible correct solutions to all the possible problems that may arise in it.

This ideal and harmonious state of affairs was sometimes imagined as a Garden of Eden before the Fall of Man, an Eden from which we were expelled, but for which we still sighed; or as a golden age still before us, in which men, having become rational, will no longer be "alienated," nor will they "alienate" or frustrate one another.

In today's societies, justice and equality are ideals that still require some degree of coercion, because the premature lifting of social controls could lead to the oppression of the weaker and more clueless by the stronger or more skilled or more energetic and unscrupulous.

But it is only the irrationality of men (according to this doctrine) that leads them to want to oppress or exploit or humiliate one another.

Rational men will respect the principle of reason in others, and will lack any desire to fight or dominate one another.

The desire to dominate is itself a symptom of irrationality, and can be explained and cured by rational methods. Spinoza offers one kind of explanation and remedy, Hegel another, Marx a third.

Some of these theories may perhaps, to some extent, complement each other, others are not combinable. But they all assume that in a society of perfectly rational beings the craving for domination over men will be absent or ineffective.

The existence or craving for oppression will be the first symptom that the true solution of the problems of social life has not been reached.

This can be expressed in another way: Freedom is self-mastery, the removal of obstacles to my will, whatever they may be: the resistance of nature, of my ungoverned passions, of irrational institutions, of opposing wills, or of the behavior of others.

"At least in principle, I can always shape nature by technical means and adapt it to my will. But how am I to deal with human beings averse to this idea? If I can, I must also impose my will on them, "mold" them according to my model, give them roles in my work. But will this not mean that I alone am free, while they are slaves?"

"They will be if my plan has nothing to do with their desires or values, only with mine. But if my plan is fully rational, it will allow the full development of their 'true' natures, the realization of their capacities to make rational decisions, to 'bring out the best in themselves', as part of the realization of my own 'true' self."

"All true solutions to all genuine problems must be compatible: more than that, they must fit into a single whole; for that is what is meant when it is said that all are rational and that the universe is harmonious. Each man has his specific character, his capacities, his aspirations, his ends. If I understand what those ends and natures are, and how they all relate to each other, I can, at least in principle, if I have the knowledge and the strength, satisfy them all, provided the nature and ends in question are rational."

"Rationality is knowing things and people for what they are: I must not use stones to make violins, nor try to make born violinists play the flute. If the universe is governed by reason, then there will be no need for coercion; a properly planned life for all will coincide with full freedom - the freedom of rational self-direction - for all."

"This will be so if, and only if, the plan is the true plan, the only model that meets the demands of reason."

"Its laws will be the rules that reason prescribes: they will only seem troublesome to those whose reason is asleep, who do not understand the true "needs" of their own "real" self."

"As long as each actor recognizes and plays the role assigned to him by reason - the faculty that understands his true nature and discerns his true ends - there can be no conflict. Each man will be a liberated and self-directed actor in the cosmic drama."

Thus Spinoza tells us that children, though coerced, are not slaves, because they obey orders given in their own interest, and that the subject of a true commonwealth is not a slave, because the common interests must include his own.

Similarly, Locke says that "where there is no law there is no liberty," because rational law is a direction to a man's "self-interest" or "general good"; and he adds that since law of this kind is that which "protects us only from bogs and precipices," it "ill deserves the name of confinement," and he speaks of desires to escape from it as irrational, forms of "license," as "brutal," and so on.

Montesquieu, forgetting his liberal moments, speaks of political liberty not as permission to do what we will, or even what the law permits, but only "the power to do what we ought to will," which Kant virtually repeats identically.

Burke proclaims the "right" of the individual to be restrained in his own interest, because "the presumed consent of every rational creature is in unison with the predisposed order of things."

The common assumption of these thinkers (and of many schoolmen before them and Jacobins and Communists after them) is that the rational ends of our "true" natures must coincide, or be made to coincide, however violently our poor, ignorant, wishful, passionate, empirical selves may cry out against this process.

Freedom is not freedom to do what is irrational, stupid or wrong.

Forcing empirical selves to follow the right pattern is not tyranny, but liberation.

Rousseau tells me that if I freely surrender all parts of my life to society, I create an entity which, having been constructed by the equal sacrifice of all its members, cannot wish to harm any of them; in such a society, we are informed, no one can be interested in harming anyone else. "In giving myself to all, I give myself to none," "and I recover as much as I lose, with sufficient new strength to preserve my new gains."

Kant tells us that when "the individual has completely abandoned his wild and lawless freedom, to find it again, intact, in a state of dependence according to law," that alone is true freedom, "for this dependence is the work of my own will acting as legislator."

Freedom, far from being incompatible with authority, becomes virtually identical with it.

This is the thought and language of all the declarations of the rights of man in the eighteenth century, and of all those who regard society as a design constructed according to the rational laws of the wise lawgiver, or of nature, or of history, or of the Supreme Being.

Bentham, almost single-handedly, kept repeating tenaciously that the aim of laws was not to liberate, but to restrict: every law is an infringement of liberty, even if such infringement leads to an increase in the sum of liberty.

If the underlying assumptions had been correct-if the method of solving social problems resembled the way solutions to problems in the natural sciences are found, and if reason were what the rationalists said it was-all this would perhaps follow.

In the ideal case, freedom coincides with law: autonomy with authority.

A law that forbids me to do what I could not, as a sane being, conceivably wish to do, is not a restriction of my freedom.

In the ideal society, composed of entirely responsible beings, the rules, since I would hardly be aware of them, would gradually disappear.

Only one social movement dared to make this assumption explicit and to accept its consequences: that of the anarchists. But all forms of liberalism based on a rationalist metaphysics are more or less diluted versions of this creed.

In due course, the thinkers who devoted their energies to the solution of the problem along this line were confronted with the question of how, in practice, men could be made rational in this way. It is evident that they must be educated. For the uneducated are irrational, heteronomous, and need to be coerced, if only to make life tolerable to the rational if they are to live in the same society and not be forced to retire to a desert or some Olympian height. But the uneducated cannot be expected to understand or cooperate with the purposes of their educators.

Education, says Fichte, must inevitably work in such a way that "later you will recognize the reasons for what I am doing now." Children cannot be expected to understand why they are forced to go to school, nor the ignorant-that is, for the moment, the majority of mankind-why they are made to obey laws that will presently make them rational.

Coercion is also a kind of education. You learn the great virtue of obedience to superior persons.

If you cannot understand your own interests as a rational being, I cannot be expected to consult you, or abide by your wishes, in the course of making you rational. In the end, I must force you to protect yourself against smallpox, even if you do not wish it.

Even Mill is willing to say that I can forcibly prevent a man from crossing a bridge if there is not time to warn him that it is about to collapse, because I know, or am justified in supposing, that he cannot wish to fall into the water.

Fichte knows what the uneducated German of his time wishes to be or to do better than he can know himself. The sage knows you better than you know yourself, because you are a victim of your passions, a slave living a heteronomous life, blind, unable to understand your true goals.

You want to be a human being. The goal of the state is to satisfy that desire. "Compulsion is justified by education for future insight."

The reason within me, if it is to triumph, must eliminate and suppress my "lower" instincts, my passions and desires, which make me a slave; likewise (the fatal transition from individual to social concepts is almost imperceptible) the higher elements of society - the best educated, the most rational, those "possessing the greatest insight of their time and of their people" - can exercise compulsion to rationalize the irrational sector of society. For - so Hegel, Bradley and Bosanquet have often assured us - by obeying the rational man we obey ourselves: not as we are, sunk in our ignorance and our passions, weak creatures afflicted with diseases that need a healer, wards that need a guardian, but as we could be if we were rational; as we could be even now, if only we would listen to the rational element that is, according to this hypothesis, within every human being worthy of the name.

The philosophers of "Objective Reason," from the "organic," rigid, centralized state of Fichte, to the soft, humane liberalism of T. H. Green, certainly supposed themselves to be meeting, and not resisting, the rational demands which, however inchoate, lay in the breast of every sentient being.

But I may reject such democratic optimism, and turning away from the ideological determinism of the Hegelians to some more voluntaristic philosophy, conceive the idea of imposing upon my society - for its own betterment - a plan of my own, which in my rational wisdom I have worked out; and which, unless I act on my own, perhaps against the abiding wishes of the vast majority of my fellow citizens, may never come to fruition at all. Or, abandoning the concept of reason altogether, I may conceive of myself as an inspired artist, molding men into patterns in the light of his unique vision, as painters combine colors or composers sounds; humanity is the raw material upon which I impose my creative will; though men suffer and die in the process, they are elevated thereby to a height they could never have reached without my coercive - but creative - violation of their lives.

This is the argument used by every dictator, inquisitor and bully who seeks some moral, or even aesthetic, justification for his conduct.

"I must do for men (or with them) what they cannot do for themselves, and I cannot ask their permission or consent, because they are not in a position to know what is best for them; indeed, what they permit and accept may mean a life of despicable mediocrity, or perhaps even their ruin and suicide."

Let me once again quote the true progenitor of the heroic doctrine, Fichte:

"No one has rights against reason. Man fears to subordinate his subjectivity to the laws of reason. He prefers tradition or arbitrariness." "Nevertheless, subordinate he must be."

Fichte vindicates what he calls reason; Napoleon, Carlyle or the Romantic authoritarians may worship other values and see in their establishment by force the only way to "true" freedom.

The same attitude was sharply expressed by Auguste Comte, who asked why, if we do not allow free thought in chemistry or biology, we should allow it in morals or politics.

Why? If it makes sense to speak of political truths-statements of social ends which all men, because they are men, must, once discovered, agree that they are so; and if, as Comte believed, the scientific method will reveal them in due course; then what is the case for freedom of opinion or action-at least as an end in itself, and not merely as a stimulating intellectual climate-whether for individuals or for groups? Why should any conduct be tolerated that is not authorized by the appropriate experts?

Comte put bluntly what had been implicit in the rationalist theory of politics since its ancient Greek origins. In principle, there can be only one right way of life; the wise lead it spontaneously, that is why they are called wise. The foolish must be dragged towards it by all social means within the reach of the wise; for why should demonstrable error be allowed to survive and reproduce itself?

The immature and the ignorant must be made to say to themselves, "Only the truth liberates, and the only way I can learn the truth is by blindly doing today what you who know it command or compel me to do, in the certainty that only thus will I come to your clear vision and be free as you are."

Certainly, we have moved away from our liberal beginnings. This argument, employed by Fichte in its last phase, and after him by other defenders of authority, from Victorian schoolmasters and colonial administrators to the last nationalist or communist dictator, is precisely what Stoic and Kantian morality protest most bitterly against in the name of the reason of the free individual following his own inner light.

Thus the rationalist argument, with its assumption of the one true solution, has led by steps which, if not logically valid, are historically and psychologically intelligible from an ethical doctrine of individual responsibility and individual self-perfection to an authoritarian state obedient to the directives of an elite of Platonic guardians.

What could have led to such a strange inversion - the transformation of Kant's stern individualism into something close to a pure totalitarian doctrine by thinkers some of whom claimed to be his disciples? This question is not of merely historical interest, for not a few contemporary liberals have gone through the same peculiar evolution.

It is true that Kant insisted, following Rousseau, that the capacity for rational self-direction belonged to all men; that there could be no experts in moral questions, since morality was not a matter of specialized knowledge (as the utilitarians and philosophers had held), but of the right use of a universal human faculty;

and, consequently, that what made men free was not acting in certain self-perfecting ways, to which they could be coerced, but knowing why they should do so, which no one could do for anyone or on behalf of anyone.

But even Kant, when he dealt with political questions, admitted that no law, provided it was such that I, if asked, would approve of it as a rational being, could deprive me of any part of my rational freedom. Thereby the door was thrown wide open to the rule of experts.

"I cannot consult all men on all laws all the time. Government cannot be a continual plebiscite. Besides, some men are not as well attuned to the voice of their own reason as others: some seem singularly deaf."

"If I am a legislator or ruler, I must assume that if the law I impose is rational (and I can only consult my own reason) it will automatically be approved by all the members of my society insofar as they are rational beings. For if they disapprove of it, they must therefore be irrational; then they will need to be restrained by reason: whether theirs or mine cannot matter, for the pronouncements of reason must be the same in all minds."

"I give my orders and, if you resist, I take it upon myself to repress the irrational element that is opposed in you to reason. My task would be easier if you would repress it yourself; I try to educate you to do so. But I am responsible for the public welfare; I cannot wait until all men are fully rational."

Kant may protest that the essence of the subject's freedom is that he, and he alone, has given himself the command to obey. But this is a counsel of perfection. If you do not discipline yourself, I must do it for you; and you cannot complain of lack of freedom, for the fact that Kant's rational judge has sent you to prison is proof that you have not listened to your own inner reason, that, like a child, a savage, an idiot, you are not ripe for self-direction, or are permanently incapable of it.

If this leads to despotism, even if it is by the best or the wisest - to the temple of Sarastro in The Magic Flute - it is still despotism, and yet it turns out to be identical with freedom, can it be that there is something wrong with the premises of the argument? That the basic premises themselves are flawed in some way?

Let me state them once more: first, that all men have but one true end, that of rational self-direction; second, that the ends of all rational beings must necessarily fit into a single universal and harmonious pattern, which some men may be able to discern more clearly than others; third, that all conflict, and consequently all tragedy, is due solely to the clash of reason with the irrational or the insufficiently rational-the immature and undeveloped elements of life, whether individual or communal-and that such clashes are, in principle, avoidable, and for fully rational beings, impossible; finally, that when all men have become rational, they will obey the rational laws of their own nature, which are one and the same in all of them, and will thus be both fully law-abiding and fully free.

Can it be that Socrates and the creators of the central Western tradition in ethics and politics that followed him have been wrong, for more than two millennia, to assert that virtue is not knowledge, nor freedom identical with both? That, despite governing the lives of more men than ever in its long history, not a single one of the basic assumptions of this famous view is provable or, perhaps, even true?

The search for status

There is another historically important approach to this issue which, by confusing liberty with its sisters, equality and fraternity, leads to equally illiberal conclusions.

Ever since the question was raised in the late eighteenth century, the question of "what is meant by the individual" has been asked insistently, and with increasing effect.

To the extent that I live in society, everything I do inevitably affects what others do and is affected by it. Even Mill's strenuous effort to mark the distinction between the spheres of private life and social life crumbles on examination.

Virtually all of Mill's critics have pointed out that everything I do can have results that harm other human beings. Moreover, I am a social being in a deeper sense than that of interaction with others. Am I not what I am, to some extent, by virtue of what others think and feel I am?

When I ask myself what I am, and answer: an Englishman, a Chinaman, a merchant, a man of no consequence, a millionaire, a convict, I discover on analysis that possessing these attributes implies being recognized as belonging to a particular group or class by others in my society, and that this recognition forms part of the meaning of most of the terms denoting some of my more personal and permanent characteristics.

I am not disembodied reason. Nor am I Robinson Crusoe, alone on his island. It is not only that my material life depends on interaction with other men, or that I am what I am as a result of social forces, but that some, perhaps all, of my ideas about myself, in particular my sense of my own moral and social identity, are intelligible only in terms of the social network in which I am (one should not strain the metaphor too much) an element.

The lack of freedom of which men or groups complain amounts, more often than not, to a lack of adequate recognition.

I may not seek what Mill would wish me to seek, i.e., security from coercion, arbitrary detention, tyranny, deprivation of certain opportunities for action, or a space within which I am legally accountable to no one for my movements.

Similarly, I may not seek a rational plan of social life or the self-perfection of a dispassionate sage.

In short, that I am not treated as an individual, that my uniqueness is not sufficiently recognized, that I am classified as a member of a featureless amalgam, a statistical unit with no identifiable, specifically human traits or purpose of my own.

This is the degradation I fight against: I seek not equal legal rights, not the freedom to do what I want (though I may want this too), but a status in which I can feel that I am, because I am considered to be, a responsible agent, whose will is taken into account because I am entitled to it, even if I am attacked and persecuted for being what I am or choosing what I do.

It is a craving for status and recognition: "The poorest there is in England has a life to live; exactly the same as the richest."

"I wish to be understood and recognized, even if it means being unpopular and disagreeable. And the only people who can recognize me and thus give me a sense of being somebody are the members of the society to which, historically, morally, morally, economically, and perhaps ethnically, I feel I belong."

"My individual self is not something I can separate from my relationship to others, or from those attributes of myself that consist in their attitude toward me. Therefore, when I demand to be freed from, say, the status of political or social dependence, what I demand is an alteration in the attitude toward me of those whose opinions and behavior contribute to determine my own self-image."

And what holds for the individual holds for groups, social, political, economic, religious, that is, for men conscious of the needs and purposes they have as members of such groups.

What oppressed classes or nationalities demand, as a rule, is not simply untrammeled freedom of action for their members, nor, above all else, equality of social or economic opportunity, still less the allocation of a place in an organic and frictionless State devised by the rational legislator. What they want, more often than not, is simply recognition (of their class or nation or color or race) as an independent source of human activity, as an entity with a will of its own, intending to act in accordance with it (whether good or legitimate, or not), and not to be governed, educated, guided, however lightly handed, as not quite human, and therefore not quite free.

This gives a much broader meaning than the purely rationalist one to Kant's observation that paternalism is "the greatest despotism imaginable."

Paternalism is despotic, not because it is more oppressive than naked, brutal, unenlightened tyranny, nor simply because it ignores the transcendental reason embodied in me, but because it is an insult to my conception of myself as a human being, determined to make my own life according to my own (not necessarily rational or benevolent) purposes and, above all, entitled to be recognized as such by others.

For if I am not so recognized, then I may not recognize, I may doubt, my own claim to be a fully independent human being. For what I am is, to a large extent, determined by what I feel and think; and what I feel and think is determined by the feeling and thinking prevailing in the society to which I belong, of which, in Burke's sense, I form not an isolable atom, but an ingredient (to use a dangerous but indispensable metaphor) in a social pattern.

I may feel unfree in the sense of not being recognized as a self-governing individual human being; but I may also feel it as a member of an unrecognized or insufficiently respected group: then

I desire the emancipation of my whole class, or community, or nation, or race, or profession.

So much may I desire this, that I may, in my bitter longing for status, prefer to be bullied and misruled by some member of my own race or social class, by whom, however, I am recognized as a man and a rival - that is, as an equal - to being well and tolerantly treated by someone of some superior and more distant group, someone who does not recognize me for what I wish to feel myself to be. This is the core of the great clamor for recognition, both by individuals and groups and, in our day, professions and classes, nations and races.

Even if I do not obtain "negative" freedom at the hands of the members of my own society, they are members of my own group; they understand me, as I understand them; and this understanding creates in me a sense of being somebody in the world.

It is this desire for reciprocal recognition that makes the most authoritarian democracies sometimes consciously preferred by their members to the most enlightened oligarchies, or that sometimes makes a member of some newly liberated Asian or African state complain less today, when he is treated rudely by members of his own race or nation, than when he was ruled by some prudent, just, gentle and well-meaning administrator from outside.

Unless this phenomenon is understood, the ideals and behavior of whole peoples who, in Mill's sense of the word, suffer deprivation of elementary human rights, and who, with all appearance of sincerity, speak of enjoying more freedom than when they possessed a larger measure of these rights, becomes an unintelligible paradox. Yet it is not with individual freedom, either in the "negative" sense or in the "positive" sense of the word, that this desire for status and recognition can easily be identified.

It is something no less profoundly necessary and for which human beings passionately strive - it is something akin to freedom, but not in itself; although it implies negative freedom for the whole group, it is more closely related to solidarity, fraternity, mutual understanding, the need for association on equal terms, all of which are sometimes - but misleadingly - called social freedom.

Social and political terms are necessarily vague. The attempt to make the vocabulary of politics too precise may render it useless. But it is no service to truth to loosen the usage beyond what is necessary.

The essence of the notion of freedom, in both the "positive" and the "negative" sense, is the containment of something or someone - of others who invade my field or assert their authority over me, or of obsessions, fears, neuroses, irrational forces - intruders and despots of one kind or another.

The desire for recognition is a desire for something different: for union, for closer understanding, for integration of interests, for a life of common dependence and sacrifice. It is only the confusion of the desire for freedom with this deep and universal longing for status and understanding, confused moreover by being identified with the notion of social self-direction, where the self to be liberated is no longer the individual but the "social whole," that makes it possible for men, while submitting to the authority of oligarchs or dictators, to pretend that this in some sense liberates them.

Much has been written about the fallacy of regarding social groups as literally persons or selves, whose control and discipline of their members is nothing more than self-discipline, voluntary self-control that leaves the individual agent free. But even from the "organic" point of view, would it be natural or desirable to call the demand for recognition and status a demand for freedom in any sense?

It is true that the group from which recognition is sought must have a sufficient measure of "negative" freedom (from control by any external authority), otherwise recognition by the group will not grant the claimant the status he seeks. But is the struggle for higher status, the desire to escape from an inferior position, a struggle for freedom? Is it mere pedantry to limit this word to the main senses discussed above, or are we, as I suspect, in danger of calling any improvement in his social status favored by a human being an increase in his freedom, and will this not render this term so vague and distended as to render it practically useless?

And yet we cannot simply dismiss this case as a mere confusion of the notion of freedom with that of status, or solidarity, or fraternity, or equality, or some combination of these.

The yearning for status is, in certain respects, very close to the desire to be an independent agent.

We can deny this goal the title of freedom; however, it would be a superficial view to assume that the analogies between individuals and groups, or the organic metaphors, or the various senses of the word "freedom," are mere fallacies, due either to claims of similarity between entities in respects in which they are different, or to simple semantic confusion.

What those who are willing to truncate their own individual freedom of action and that of others for the status of their group, and their own status within the group, want is not simply a renunciation of freedom for the sake of security, of an assured place in a harmonious hierarchy in which all men and all classes know their place, and are willing to exchange the painful privilege of choice-"the burden of freedom"-for the peace and comfort and relative meaninglessness of an authoritarian or totalitarian structure.

There is no doubt that there are such men and such desires, and there is no doubt that such renunciations of individual freedom can and, indeed, often have occurred. But it is a profound misunderstanding of the temper of our time to suppose that this is what makes nationalism or Marxism attractive to nations that have been ruled by foreign masters, or to classes whose lives were run by other classes in a semi-feudal regime, or in some other hierarchically organized regime.

What they seek is more akin to what Mill called "pagan self-assertion," but in a collective and socialized form.

Indeed, much of what he says about his own reasons for desiring freedom-the value he places on boldness and nonconformism, on the assertion of the individual's own values in the face of prevailing opinion, on strong, self-reliant personalities free from the shackles of society's lawmakers and official instructors-has little to do with his conception of freedom as noninterference, but has much to do with men's desire not to have the value of their personality too much lowered, to be regarded as incapable of autonomous, original, "authentic" behavior, even if such behavior should be subject to opprobrium, social restraint, or inhibiting legislation.

This desire to assert the "personality" of my class, group, or nation, is related both to the answer to the question "What should be the sphere of authority?" (since the group should not be interfered with by external masters) and, even more closely, to the answer to the question "Who should rule us?" -govern well or badly, liberally or oppressively, but above all "Who?".

And answers like "Elected representatives by my own and others' choice," or "All of us gathered in regular assemblies," or "The best," or "The wisest," or "The nation embodied in these or those persons or institutions," or "The divine leader" are answers that are logically, and sometimes also politically and socially, independent of the degree of "negative" freedom I demand for my own or my group's activities.

As long as the answer to "Who governs me?" is someone or something that I can represent as "mine," as something that belongs to me or to which I belong, I can, using words that convey fraternity and solidarity, as well as part of the connotation of the "positive" sense of the word "freedom" (which is difficult to specify more precisely), describe it as a hybrid form of freedom; in any case, as an ideal that is perhaps more prominent than any other in the world today, but to which no existing term seems to fit precisely.

Those who buy it status at the price of their "negative" freedom certainly claim to be "liberated" by this means, in this confused, but ardently felt sense.

"Whose service is perfect freedom" can be secularized in this way, and the State, or the nation, or the race, or an assembly, or a dictator, or my family or my environment, or myself, can be substituted for the Deity, without thereby the word "freedom" losing all meaning.

Surely, any interpretation of the word "freedom," however unusual, must include a minimum of what I have called "negative" freedom. There must be a realm within which I do not feel frustrated. No society suppresses literally all the liberties of its members; a being who is prevented by others from doing anything for himself is not a moral agent at all, and could not be regarded either legally or morally as a human being, even if a physiologist or a biologist, or even a psychologist, were inclined to classify him as a man.

But the fathers of liberalism-Mill and Constant-want more than this minimum: they demand a maximum degree of non-interference compatible with the minimum requirements of social life.

It seems unlikely that this extreme demand for freedom has ever been formulated by anyone other than a small minority of highly civilized and self-conscious human beings.

Most of mankind has certainly been willing on most occasions to sacrifice it for the sake of other goals: security, status, prosperity, power, virtue, otherworldly rewards; or justice, equality, fraternity and many other values that seem wholly or partially incompatible with the attainment of the highest degree of individual freedom, and which certainly do not need it as a precondition for their own realization.

It is not the demand for a "Lebensraum" for each individual that has stimulated the rebellions and wars of liberation for which men have been willing to die in the past or, indeed, in the present. Men who have fought for freedom have commonly fought for the right to be governed by themselves or by their representatives - governed severely, if necessary, like the Spartans, with little individual freedom, but in a way that allowed them to participate, or at least to believe that they were participating, in the legislation and administration of their collective lives. And men who have made revolutions, in most cases, have understood by freedom no more than the conquest of power and authority by a particular sect of believers in a doctrine, or by a class, or by some other social group, old or new.

Undoubtedly, their victories frustrated those whom they overthrew, and sometimes repressed, enslaved or exterminated large numbers of human beings. However, these revolutionaries have usually found it necessary to argue that, in spite of this, they represented the party of freedom, or of "true" freedom, claiming the universality of their ideal, which supposedly also sought the "real selves" even of those who resisted them, even though they were considered to have lost their way to the goal, or to have missed the wrong goal due to some moral or spiritual blindness.

All this has little to do with Mill's notion of freedom as limited only by the danger of harming others.

It is the failure to recognize this psychological and political fact (hidden behind the apparent ambiguity of the term "liberty") that has, perhaps, blinded some contemporary liberals to the world in which they live. Their plea is clear, their cause is just. But they fail to take into account the variety of basic human needs. Nor the ingenuity with which men can demonstrate to their own satisfaction that the road to an ideal also leads to its opposite.

Liberty and Sovereignty

The French Revolution, like all great revolutions, was, at least in its Jacobin form, precisely an eruption of the desire for "positive" freedom of collective self-direction on the part of a great mass of French people who felt liberated as a nation, even if the result was, for a good part of them, a severe restriction of individual liberties.

Rousseau had spoken exultantly that the laws of liberty could be more austere than the yoke of tyranny.

Tyranny is the service of human masters. The law cannot be tyrannical. Rousseau does not mean by liberty the "negative" freedom of the individual not to be interfered with within a defined sphere, but the possession by all, and not only by some, of the fully qualified members of a society of a share of the public power which has the right to interfere in all aspects of the life of every citizen.

The liberals of the first half of the nineteenth century correctly foresaw that liberty in this "positive" sense could easily destroy too many of the "negative" liberties they held sacred. They pointed out that the sovereignty of the people could easily destroy that of individuals.

Mill explained, patiently and incontestably, that the government of the people was not, in their sense, necessarily liberty. For the rulers are not necessarily the same "people" as the ruled, and democratic self-government is not the government "of each for himself," but, at best, "of each for all the rest."

Mill and his disciples spoke of "the tyranny of the majority" and the tyranny of "dominant opinion and sentiment," and saw little difference between the latter and any other kind of tyranny that encroaches upon the activities of men beyond the sacred boundaries of private life.

No one saw the conflict between the two kinds of liberty better, nor expressed it more clearly, than Benjamin Constant.

He pointed out that the transfer by a successful uprising of unlimited authority, commonly called sovereignty, from one set of hands to another does not increase liberty, but merely shifts the burden of slavery.

He reasonably wondered why a man should care deeply about being crushed by a popular government or by a monarch, or even by an oppressive set of laws. He saw that the main problem for those who desire "negative" individual liberty is not who exercises this authority, but how much authority should be placed in the hands of any set of people.

In his view, unlimited authority in the hands of anyone is bound, sooner or later, to destroy someone. He held that men generally protested against this or that set of rulers as oppressors, when the real cause of oppression lay in the mere fact of the accumulation of power itself, wherever it was found, for liberty was endangered by the mere existence of absolute authority as such.

"It is not against the arm that we must lash out," he wrote, "but against the weapon." "Some burdens are too heavy for the human hand."

Democracy can disarm a given oligarchy, a given privileged individual or set of individuals, but it can still crush individuals as ruthlessly as any previous ruler.

The very right to oppress - or to interfere - does not equal freedom. Nor does universal consent to the loss of liberty miraculously preserve it merely by being universal, or by being consent.

If I consent to be oppressed or accept my condition with indifference or irony, am I any less oppressed? If I sell myself into slavery, am I less of a slave? If I commit suicide, am I less dead for having freely taken my life? "Popular government is but a spasmodic tyranny, monarchy a more centralized despotism."

Constant saw in Rousseau the most dangerous enemy of individual liberty, because he had declared that "in giving myself to all, I give myself to none." Constant did not see why, although the sovereign is "the whole world," he should not oppress one of the "members" of his indivisible being, if he so chose.

Of course, I may prefer to be deprived of my liberties by an assembly, a family, or a class in which I am a minority. It may one day give me the opportunity to persuade others to do for me what I believe I am entitled to. But to be deprived of my liberty at the hands of my family or friends or fellow citizens is to be deprived of it with exactly the same efficacy.

Hobbes was in any case more frank: he did not claim that a sovereign did not enslave; he justified this enslavement, but at least he did not have the effrontery to call it liberty.

Throughout the nineteenth century, liberal thinkers maintained that if liberty implied a limit to the powers of any man to compel me to do what I did not or could not wish to do, then, whatever the ideal in the name of which I was coerced, I was not free; that the doctrine of absolute sovereignty was a tyrannical doctrine in itself.

If I wish to preserve my liberty, it is not enough to say that it must not be violated unless someone-the absolute ruler, or the popular assembly, or the King in Parliament, or the judges, or some combination of authorities, or the laws themselves (for the laws may be oppressive)-authorizes its violation. I must establish a society in which there must be boundaries of freedom which no one must be able to cross. The norms that determine these frontiers may be given different names or natures: they may be called natural rights, or the word of God, or natural law, or the demands of utility or the "permanent interests of man"; I may believe them to be valid a priori, or claim them to be my own ultimate ends, or the ends of my society or culture. What these norms or commandments will have in common is that they are so widely accepted and so deeply rooted in the real nature of men, as they have developed over the course of history, that they are already an essential part of what we mean by being a normal human being.

Genuine belief in the inviolability of a minimum of individual freedom implies an absolute stance of this kind. For it is clear that it has little to expect from majority rule; democracy as such is not logically committed to it, and has historically failed on occasion to protect it while remaining true to its own principles.

Few governments, it has been observed, have found difficulty in making their subjects flourish the will that the government wanted.

The triumph of despotism consists in compelling slaves to declare themselves free. Force may not be necessary; slaves may proclaim their freedom in all sincerity: but they do not cease to be slaves.

Perhaps the main value to liberals of political - "positive" - rights to participate in government is as a means of protecting what they consider an ultimate value, namely, individual - "negative" - liberty.

But if democracies can, while remaining democratic, suppress freedom, at least as liberals have used the word, what would make a society truly free?

For Constant, Mill, Tocqueville and the liberal tradition to which they belong, no society is free unless it is governed by at least two interrelated principles:

First, that no power, but only rights, can be considered absolute, so that all men, whatever power governs them, have an absolute right to refuse to behave inhumanely; and, secondly, that there are boundaries, not artificially drawn, within which men must be inviolable, these boundaries being defined in terms of rules so long and widely accepted that their observance has entered into the very conception of what it is to be a normal human being and, therefore, also of what it is to act inhumanely or insanely; rules of which it would be absurd to say, for example, that they could be abrogated by some formal procedure on the part of some court or sovereign body.

When I speak of a man being normal, I mean in part that he could not easily break these rules, without a shudder of revulsion. It is these rules that are broken when a man is convicted without trial, or punished under a retroactive law; when children are ordered to denounce their parents, friends to betray one another, soldiers to use barbarous methods; when men are tortured or murdered, or minorities are massacred because they irritate a majority or a tyrant.

Such acts, even if legalized by the sovereign, cause horror even in these days, and this arises from the recognition of the moral validity - irrespective of laws - of some absolute barriers to the imposition of one man's will upon another.

The freedom of a society, of a class or of a group, in this sense of freedom, is measured by the strength of these barriers and by the number and importance of the paths they keep open for their members, if not for all, at any rate for a large number of them.

This is almost at the opposite pole of the purposes of those who believe in freedom in the "positive" -self-directive- sense.

The former -defenders of negative freedom- want to curb authority as such. The latter -defenders of positive freedom- want to put it in their own hands.

This is a cardinal question. It is not a question of two different interpretations of the same concept, but of two profoundly divergent and irreconcilable attitudes towards the ends of life.

It is convenient to recognize this, even if in practice it is often necessary to reach a compromise between them. Each has absolute claims. Both cannot be fully satisfied. But it is a profound lack of social and moral understanding not to recognize that the satisfaction each seeks is an ultimate value which, both historically and morally, has an equal right to be ranked among the deepest interests of humanity.

The One and the Many

One belief, more than any other, is responsible for the slaughter of individuals on the altars of great historical ideals - justice or progress or the happiness of future generations, or the sacred mission or emancipation of a nation or race or class, or even freedom itself, which demands the sacrifice of individuals for the freedom of society. It is the belief that somewhere, in the past or in the future, in divine revelation or in the mind of an individual thinker, in the pronouncements of history or science, or in the simple heart of an uncorrupted good man, there is an ultimate solution to the problems of society.

This ancient faith rests on the conviction that all the positive values in which men have believed must, in the end, be compatible, and perhaps even mutually implicate each other.

"Nature unites truth, happiness and virtue by an indissoluble chain," said one of the greatest men who ever lived - Aristotle - and he spoke in similar terms of freedom, equality and justice.

But is this true? It is a commonplace that neither political equality, nor efficient organization, nor social justice are compatible with more than a minimum of individual liberty, and certainly not with unrestricted laissez-faire; that justice and generosity, public and private loyalties, the demands of genius and the demands of society may come into violent conflict with each other. And from there to the generalization that not all good things are compatible, let alone all the ideals of humanity, there is no great stretch.

But somewhere, we will be told, and somehow, it must be possible for all these values to coexist, for if it is not so, the universe is not a cosmos, not a harmony; if it is not so, conflicts of values may be an intrinsic and immovable element of human life.

To admit that the realization of some of our ideals can, in principle, make impossible the realization of others is to say that the notion of total human fulfillment is a formal contradiction, a metaphysical chimera.

For every rationalist metaphysician, from Plato to the latest disciples of Hegel or Marx, this abandonment of the notion of a final harmony in which all enigmas are solved, all contradictions reconciled, is a piece of crude empiricism, an abdication before brute facts, an intolerable bankruptcy of reason before things as they are, an inability to explain and justify, to reduce everything to a system, which "reason" indignantly rejects.

But if we are not armed with an a priori warrant for the proposition that a total harmony of true values lies somewhere-perhaps in some ideal realm whose characteristics we cannot, in our finite state, even conceive of-we must fall back on the ordinary resources of empirical observation and ordinary human knowledge. And certainly these give us no warrant for supposing (or even understanding what it would mean to say) that all things good, or all things bad, are reconcilable with each other.

The world we encounter in ordinary experience is a world in which we are faced with choices between equally ultimate ends, and equally absolute claims, the realization of some of which must inevitably involve the sacrifice of others. Indeed, if they were assured that in some perfect state, realizable by men on earth, no end pursued by them would ever conflict, the necessity and agony of choice would disappear, and with them the central importance of the freedom to choose. Any method of approaching this final state would then seem fully justified, no matter how much freedom would be sacrificed to advance toward it.

I have no doubt that such a dogmatic certainty has been responsible for the deep, serene and unshakable conviction in the minds of some of history's most ruthless tyrants and persecutors that what they were doing was fully justified by their purpose.

I do not say that the ideal of self-perfection-whether for individuals or nations or Churches or classes-is in itself reprehensible, or that the language used in its defense was in every case the result of a confused or fraudulent use of words, or of moral or intellectual perversity. In fact, I have tried to show that it is the notion of freedom in its "positive" sense that lies at the heart of the demands for national or social self-direction that animate the most powerful and morally just public movements of our time, and that not to recognize this is to misunderstand the most vital facts and ideas of our time. But it also seems to me that the belief that a single formula can be found in principle for harmoniously realizing the various ends of men is manifestly false.

If, as I believe, men's ends are many, and not all of them are in principle compatible with one another, then the possibility of conflict - and of tragedy - can never be entirely eliminated from human life, either personal or social.

The need to choose between absolute claims is thus an inescapable characteristic of the human condition. This gives its value to freedom as Acton conceived it: as an end in itself, and not as a temporary necessity, arising from our confused notions and our irrational and disordered lives, a predicament that a panacea might one day fix.

I do not mean that individual freedom is, even in the most liberal societies, the only criterion for social action, or even the dominant one.

We force the education of children and prohibit public executions. Undoubtedly, these are restrictions on freedom. And we justify them on the grounds that ignorance, a barbarous education, or cruel pleasures and excitements are worse for us than the amount of restraint necessary to repress them.

This judgment depends in turn on how we determine right and wrong, that is, on our moral, religious, intellectual, economic and aesthetic values; which are, in turn, linked to our conception of man and the basic demands of his nature.

In other words, our solution to such problems is based on our vision, by which we are consciously or unconsciously guided, of what constitutes a full human life, in contrast to Mill's "shrunken and dwarfed", "reduced and corseted" natures.

To protest against laws governing censorship or personal morality as intolerable infringements of personal freedom presupposes the belief that the activities such laws prohibit are fundamental needs of men as men, in a good (or, indeed, any) society.

To defend such laws is to hold that these needs are not essential, or that they cannot be satisfied without sacrificing other values that are above - satisfy deeper needs - individual freedom, determined by some standard that is not merely subjective, a standard for which some objective - empirical or a priori - status is claimed.

The extent of a man's, or a people's, freedom to choose to live as he wishes must be weighed against the claims of many other values, of which equality, or justice, or happiness, or security, or public order are perhaps the most obvious examples. For this reason, it cannot be unlimited. R. H. Tawney rightly reminds us that the freedom of the strong, whether their physical or economic strength, must be restricted.

This maxim demands respect, not as a consequence of some a priori rule, according to which respect for the freedom of one man logically entails respect for the freedom of others like him; but simply because respect for the principles of justice, or shame in the face of gross inequality of treatment, is as basic in men as the desire for freedom.

That we cannot have it all is a necessary, not a contingent, truth. Burke's plea for the constant need to compensate, reconcile, and balance; Mill's plea for new "experiments in life" with their permanent possibility of error-the knowledge that it is not only in practice but in principle impossible to reach clear and certain answers, even in an ideal world of wholly good and rational men and wholly clear ideas-may drive mad those who seek definitive solutions and single all-encompassing systems, guaranteed to be eternal. Yet it is a conclusion from which those who, with Kant, have learned the truth that "from the crooked trunk of humanity nothing straight was ever made."

There is no need to insist on the fact that monism, and faith in a single criterion, have always proved to be a deep source of satisfaction both to the intellect and to the emotions. Whether the standard of judgment derives from the vision of some future perfection, as in the minds of the philosophers of the eighteenth century and their technocratic successors of our own day, or whether it is rooted in the past - la terre et les morts - as the German historicists or the French theocrats, or the neoconservatives of the Anglo-Saxon countries maintain, it is bound, provided it is sufficiently inflexible, to meet with some unforeseen and unforeseeable human development, to which it will not conform; and then it will be used to justify the a priori barbarities of Procrusteus: the vivisection of real human societies into some fixed pattern dictated by our fallible understanding of a largely imaginary past or a wholly imaginary future.

Preserving our absolute categories or ideals at the expense of human lives offends the principles of science and history alike; it is an attitude found in equal measure on the right and left wings in our day, and is not reconcilable with the principles accepted by those who respect facts.

Pluralism, with the measure of "negative" freedom it entails, seems to me a truer and more humane ideal than the aims of those who seek in the great disciplined and authoritarian structures the ideal of the "positive" self-mastery of classes, or of peoples, or of all mankind.

It is truer because, at least, it recognizes the fact that human objectives are many, not all commensurable and in perpetual rivalry with one another.

To assume that all values can be ranked on a scale, so that it is a mere matter of inspection to determine the highest, seems to me to falsify our knowledge that men are free agents, to represent moral decision as an operation which, in principle, could be performed by a slide rule.

To say that in some ultimate, all-reconciling but realizable synthesis, duty is interest, or individual freedom is pure democracy or an authoritarian state, is to throw a metaphysical blanket over self-deception or deliberate hypocrisy.

The ideal of negative freedom is more humane because it does not (as the system-builders do) deprive men, in the name of some remote or incoherent ideal, of much of what they have found indispensable to their lives as unpredictably self-transforming human beings.

In the end, men choose among ultimate values; they choose as they choose because their life and thought are determined by fundamental moral categories and concepts that are, in any case over great stretches of time and space, part of their being and thought and sense of their own identity; part of what makes them human.

It may be that the ideal of freedom to choose ends without claiming eternal validity for them, and the related pluralism of values, is only the late fruit of our declining capitalist civilization: an ideal that remote ages and primitive societies have not recognized, and that posterity will look upon with curiosity, even sympathy, but with little understanding. This may be so; but no skeptical conclusion seems to me to follow from it.

Principles are no less sacred because their duration cannot be guaranteed.

Indeed, the very desire to have assurances that our values are eternal and secure in some objective heaven is perhaps only a longing for the certainties of childhood or the absolute values of our primitive past.

"What distinguishes a civilized man from a barbarian is to be aware of the relative validity of his convictions," said an admirable writer of our time, "and yet to defend them without hesitation."- Joseph Schumpeter.

To demand more than this is perhaps a deep and incurable metaphysical necessity; but to allow it to determine one's practice is symptomatic of an equally deep and more dangerous moral and political immaturity.

More books you might be interested in:

ECONOMIC CALCULATION IN THE SOCIALIST COMMONWEALTH: A critique of the non-existent price system of the centralized communist economy

By Ludwig von Mises

Made in the USA
Monee, IL
08 May 2025